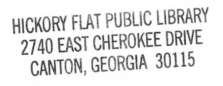

A Day With a
Cheyenne

A CHEYENNE

by Franco Meli

Illustrations by Giorgio Bacchin
Translated by Dominique Clift

RP

Runestone Press/Minneapolis
A Division of the Lerner Publishing Group

All words that appear in **bold** are explained in the
glossary that starts on page 43.

This edition first published in the United States in 1999 by Runestone Press.

Runestone Press, A Division of the Lerner Publishing Group
241 First Avenue North, Minneapolis, MN 55401 U.S.A.

website: www.lernerbooks.com

Photos are used courtesy of Franco Meli, Milan, Italy, p. 8 (top), p. 9 (top);
Colorado Historical Society, p. 8 (bottom left), The Southwest Museum, p. 9
(bottom right); The Oklahoma Historical Society, p. 15 (top right); American
Indian Art Magazine (vol. 14, no.4, Autumn 1989), p. 12 (top), p. 13 (top left);
Denver Art Museum, p. 12 (bottom), p. 13 (bottom); Grinnell, G.B. *The
Cheyenne Indians: Their History and Ways of Life, Vol. 1.* (Lincoln, NB: University
of Nebraska Press, 1972), p. 13 (top right), p. 14 (top left and bottom left);
Granata Press, Milan, Italy /IFA, pp. 14-15 (top middle). Additional Artwork
from Jaca Book, Milan, Italy (Cristina Tralli), p. 10, p. 11.

Library of Congress Cataloging-in-Publication Data

Meli, Franco.
[Giornata con un Cheyenne. English]
A Cheyenne / by Franco Meli ; illustrations by Giorgio Bacchin;
translated by Dominique Clift.
p. cm. — (A day with)
Includes bibliographical references and index.
Summary: Uses factual information and a fictional story to
describe the daily life of the Cheyenne Indians living along the
banks of the Powder River in Montana.
Half title: Day with a Cheyenne.
ISBN 0-8225-1920-8 (lib. bdg. : alk. paper)
1. Cheyenne Indians—Juvenile literature. [1. Cheyenne Indians.
2. Indians of North America—Montana.] I. Title.
II. Title: Day with a Cheyenne. III. Series.
E99.C53M4413 1999
978'.004973—dc21   99-19389

Manufactured in the United States of America
1 2 3 4 5 6 — JR — 04 03 02 01 00 99

CONTENTS

INTRODUCTION

The ancestors of Native Americans, also called American Indians, inhabited North America before Europeans arrived in the 1500s. North America ranges from tropical (hot and lush) to arctic (cold and snowy) in climate. Bounded by oceans to the east and west, the continent is crossed by wild rivers and lined with jutting mountain ranges. Plains stretch across North America, and huge lakes dot its surface. Deserts and woodlands spread over many regions.

Early Native American cultures adapted to the environments in which they lived. In coastal regions, Native Americans hunted sea creatures and collected shellfish from the ocean waters. Inland river and lake Indians netted or speared freshwater fish in creeks, lakes, and rivers. On the wide, grassy plains, Native Americans hunted buffalo by throwing spears, by shooting arrows, or by luring the animals over cliffs. In the forests, some folks hunted deer and small mammals. In other parts of the continent, farmers grew corn, beans, and squash in small plots or large areas. Houses and clothing varied, too.

Native American belief systems also reflected environments. Many belief systems were **animist,** which gave every object a spirit. Some religions revolved around animals and successful hunting, the weather, the changing seasons, or the ocean.

Over centuries, Native Americans traveled from one end of the continent to the other and sometimes back again. These movements are remembered in the oral histories of many Indian nations and can be traced in the groups of languages that people speak. Ancient American Indians spoke more than 200 distinct languages, with thousands of dialects.

Some North American civilizations grew into huge empires ruled by powerful leaders. Large populations flooded cities that were later deserted. Small towns and villages flourished, as did **nomadic** communities. No one was rich or poor in some cultures, but in others rich members lived in splendor while their poor neighbors shivered in small dwellings.

Trade routes linked people across the continent, bringing goods and new ideas from faraway places. The idea of pottery traveled from modern-day Mexico to what would later become the southwestern United States. Other people may have traded **buffalo** hides or meat for farm produce.

The Cheyenne lived in **tepees** along the rivers of the **Great Plains.** They hunted large herds of buffalo. This story, set sometime between 1740 and 1864, describes the daily life of the Cheyenne who lived on the Powder River in what would become southeastern Montana.

Series Editors

PART ONE

THE WORLD
OF THE CHEYENNE

The Cheyenne are a legendary people. As a strong presence in what came to be known as the western United States, the Cheyenne played a leading role in the defense of Native American territory against the western expansion of the U.S. government.

The Cheyenne are best known for this phase of armed encounters, which include the Massacre of Sand Creek in 1864 and the Battle of the Little Bighorn in 1876. Accounts of such violent warfare, readily found in history books, strike the collective imagination and fit stereotypes of Native Americans as warring peoples. But that is only a small part of Cheyenne culture. The story of the Cheyenne people and their way of life is much more complex.

The Cheyenne were a small group of peaceful people who once survived on small game, berries, and roots along the Minnesota River. After suffering attacks from larger groups such as the **Cree** and the **Sioux,** the group moved west to the Great Plains, an area of vast, wide-open grasslands. The Cheyenne eventually settled in the Black Hills region of modern-day South Dakota around 1740. In later years, the Cheyenne thrived in what would become the states of Nebraska, Colorado, Wyoming, Kansas, Montana, and Oklahoma.

(Facing page top) A view of the Little Bighorn River in southeastern Montana shows the site of the Battle of the Little Bighorn. (Facing page, bottom) This drawing by Robert Lindneux depicts the Massacre of Sand Creek of 1864. (Below center) An engraving, which appeared in a 1868 issue of Harper's Weekly, *shows Custer's Seventh Cavalry attacking a Cheyenne village on the Washita River in southwestern Oklahoma. (Below right) After the Battle of the Little Bighorn, illustrated here by Kicking Bear, U.S. efforts to end "hostilities" in the western territories intensified. When the government established two reservations in 1884—one in Oklahoma and the other in Montana— Cheyenne independence ended. (Above) The Massacre of Sand Creek took place in the fields of northeastern Colorado.*

Deerskin dresses—lavishly decorated with shells, glass beads, and embossed metal pieces obtained through trade—were the typical attire of southern Cheyenne women living in Oklahoma in 1890.

The Cheyenne quickly adapted to life on the plains. They hunted the larger game that roamed the area and became increasingly dependent on the buffalo. Buffalo meat and **tallow** (fat) could be cooked over an open fire and eaten fresh or dried in the sun and stored for later consumption. The Cheyenne tanned the buffalo hides and used the leather to make ropes, bags, and other useful items. **Travois** (sleds made by wrapping untanned buffalo hides around long, thin, willow poles) were pulled behind horses and used to haul meat from a hunt or goods for trade. Women created spoons, bowls, and other utensils and tools from the animal's bones.

When the Sioux formed an alliance with the Cheyenne in the late eighteenth century, they introduced the Cheyenne to tepees. Made by staking several long pine poles in a circle and tying their tops together high above the circle's center, tepee frames were then draped in buffalo skins. These cone-shaped dwellings suited the new plains lifestyle of the Cheyenne because the homes could be easily moved to different locations. As Cheyenne hunters followed buffalo herds around the plains, their families could accompany them. The Cheyenne built fires in the middle of their dwellings to keep warm in the winter, so builders left an opening in the tepee top that served as a chimney. A flap of buffalo skin could be pulled across the opening at the top when the fire pit was not in use. Around the fire pits, Cheyenne women placed thick mats of buffalo fur to be used as beds or as seating. When the **tribe** planned to stay in an area for a while, Cheyenne women decorated the family dwellings with more elaborate furnishings. They fashioned raised benches out of sod to arrange around the fire pit and created cupboards from buffalo furs and twigs.

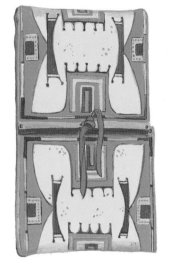

(Top left) *Dating from about 1870, this decorated rawhide shield demonstrates the importance of the buffalo in Cheyenne culture.* (Top middle) **Parfleches**—*rectangular, rawhide containers folded like envelopes—were used to transport dry food, blankets, and tools.* (Above) *The rectangle on this map of North America marks the Great Plains region.* (Left) *This map of the U.S. Great Plains region pinpoints sites of the most important events in Cheyenne history and the location of the two reservations where many Cheyenne still live.*

Drawings made in 1876 by Howling Wolf, a Cheyenne warrior held prisoner at Fort Marion in Florida, capture the life of the Plains Indians before they were confined to reservations. The image on the far right depicts the buffalo hunt and the activities surrounding it. The illustration on the immediate right features a U.S. delegation's visit to a neighboring group. Richard Pratt, commander of Fort Marion, encouraged prisoners to produce works to sell to tourists who visited the fort. (Below) This **medicine pipe** *was carved from black slate.*

Through trade with plains groups from areas farther south, such as the **Comanche** and the **Kiowa,** the Cheyenne acquired horses. Introduced to North America by the Spanish **conquistadors,** these animals greatly improved Cheyenne hunting techniques and transformed the men into effective warriors, who came to be feared by neighboring groups. The Cheyenne trained their horses to ride very close to prey, which freed up both of the hunter's hands for shooting arrows. In Cheyenne culture, horses rose to such prominence that a good war pony was considered a man's most cherished possession. Because horses were so valuable, stealing them from other tribes was encouraged and thought of as a noble deed demanding great courage and skill. In fact, horse stealing, hunting, and fighting were all used to test the bravery

(Above right) *Cheyenne warriors wore shields, like this one adorned with eagle feathers, off the right arm and used them to ward off arrows. The shield was also believed to offer spiritual protection.* (Right) *Deerskin boots adorned with glass beads arranged in a complex geometrical design kept feet warm and dry during the winter months.*

and expertise of young Cheyenne men before they would be regarded as adult men. The Cheyenne believed that if a man learned how to handle weapons and to hunt early in life, he would be more likely to achieve status within the tribe when he grew older.

The most respected Cheyenne men were not warriors, but chiefs. Chiefs were responsible for maintaining peace within the tribe and with outsiders. To become a chief, a man had to be

(Above) *These photos were taken in the 1920s. The top photo shows a woman grinding wild **chokecherries** in a **mortar**. She will then mix the ground cherries with fat and finely pounded buffalo meat to make **pemmican,** a concentrated source of food enjoyed by Native Americans. In the bottom photo, a travois is hitched to a horse. (Above right) Buffalo roam across a pasture on a Montana reservation. Because of excessive hunting during western settlement, buffalo populations have dwindled over the past 300 years. In 1700 the North American buffalo population was 60 million. By 1889 only 835 remained. These days about 30,000 buffalo graze in nature reserves in Canada, Montana, Nebraska, North Dakota, South Dakota, and Oklahoma.*

calm, generous, kind, understanding, brave, and self-sacrificing. The entire Cheyenne tribe was divided into 44 bands, and each band had a chief. Chiefs led a band for 10-year terms that couldn't be revoked. Chiefs from each of the different bands formed a **village council** that governed the Cheyenne tribe. At meetings, chiefs decided important issues, such as when to move camp or whether the nation should form an alliance with another tribe.

Although Cheyenne women didn't participate in tribal government, hunting, or warfare, they did play a vital role in village life. Women fixed meals, tanned hides, sewed clothing, and gathered roots, berries, and firewood. And when a tribe moved their village to a new location, it was the women who were in charge of moving the tepees.

Women used the hides they laboriously tanned to make clothing. They used **sinew** (pieces of animal tendon) to sew long dresses for the women. For the men, they fashioned long-sleeved shirts, fringed **leggings,** and the **breechclout,** a square piece of hide

that hung from a man's waist to his mid-thigh. All Cheyenne wore moccasins, which women made by cutting a single piece of leather for the top of the shoe and sewing it to the sole, which was cut from a piece of thicker leather. Women decorated the shoes with colorful, tiny beads obtained through trade with Europeans.

Cheyenne women gathered food for the tribe. Digging for roots and gathering berries was hard work, so women headed off early in the morning in small groups, returning late in the day. Wild turnips were a staple in the Cheyenne diet, so women spent a lot of time digging them up, boiling them, slicing them, and then spreading them out in the sun to dry.

Many different kinds of berries supplemented the Cheyenne diet, the most common being the chokecherry. Women ground the cherries into a pulp in stone mortars and mixed them with tallow and dried meat to make pemmican. A solid mass of food that provided the energy needed for day-long hunts, pemmican was used as a trailmix among the Cheyenne.

(Above) *A Cheyenne drawing depicts a warrior wearing an eagle-feather headdress. Each feather represents a courageous action.*

The following story takes place in a Cheyenne village located in southeastern Montana along the Powder River. An area between the Little Missouri and Yellowstone Rivers, this country of boundless land and sky is not far from the Black Hills of South Dakota. We join the Cheyenne in the first decades of the nineteenth century, just before the most bitter and violent clashes between the Cheyenne and the white settlers occurred. During this period, white settlers had already arrived in the area, and their influence had begun to transform the Cheyenne way of life considerably.

The arrival of new hunters to the region, for example, prompted a steady decline in the number of buffalo, an animal of great dietary and cultural importance to the Cheyenne. The newcomers established trading posts that were filled with goods and foodstuffs previously unknown to Native Americans. The white settlers introduced guns, which greatly improved Cheyenne hunting techniques and became an extremely important factor in the balance of power between the settlers and the Cheyenne. Introduction to new things isn't always for the better. Alcohol had a catastrophic effect on the Cheyenne and other Native American groups.

Let's join Painted Shield, a Cheyenne hunter, and his oldest son, Gray Falcon, as they go about their daily activities on a rather unusual and exciting day in the late 1800s. Remember that although the people and the places in the story are imaginary, the geographical, historical, and social context is real.

Part Two

A Day with Painted Shield,
a Cheyenne Hunter

**A**s the light of day drove away night's blackness in the long valley of the Powder River, Painted Shield's village came to life. The village consisted of 100 tepees set in a wide circle. The season was Ponoma'haseneeeshe'he, or Drying up Moon (the month of March). At this early hour just before sunrise, the cold air still had a bite, which Painted Shield felt on his face and on his hands as he lifted the buffalo-hide flap of his tepee.

A strong wind pushed the clouds across the sky as Painted Shield put on his winter moccasins and walked toward the river for his morning prayer. He splashed his face with the cold, clear water and turned to the east, toward the sun, which had begun to brighten the earth. He gave thanks for all the elements of creation—the sun, the moon, the stars, the earth, the water, the animals, and the plants. In the tradition of his people, Painted Shield burned some aromatic **sage** to accompany his prayers. He turned to the east, to the west, to the north, and to the south to indicate that spiritual help comes from sacred powers who exist at all four directions.

Painted Shield asked **Ma'heo'o** (the Sacred One) that this hunting day be successful, for this was the day he planned to initiate his eldest son, Gray Falcon, to the hunt. Just then Gray Falcon emerged from the family tepee behind two barking, yellow dogs. Gray Falcon told his father that his mother, Morning Light, had prepared breakfast. The fire was burning in the middle of the tepee. Across the village, columns of smoke rose from the vent holes of every tent. The wind pushed the smoke toward the hills and the mountains, which stretched around them in all directions.

Once inside the tepee, Painted Shield and Gray Falcon sat down next to the fire on a pile of buffalo skins. Morning Light served a smooth and nourishing wild-cherry soup. Long Spear, Painted Shield's younger brother, appeared at the entrance of the tepee. He sat down between his two nephews, Gray Falcon and Spotted Fox.

Morning Light was well known throughout the village for her good cooking. She was also widely respected for the saddlebags she fashioned from leather and decorated with strings of pearls. Her favorite design was a diamond with a three-pronged spear in its center. Her favorite colors, made from the dye of plants and rocks she gathered, were red, light blue, and green.

After finishing his breakfast, Painted Shield turned to his son and said, "Today is a fine day to take you to the **trading post.** Then we'll go and track some *hotoa'o* (buffalo)." Gray Falcon eagerly hung on his father's every word. This was the first time his father had invited him along for a hunt.

Painted Shield continued. "This winter has been very hard. We are lucky that this past summer's hunt was plentiful. We've been able to live off the meat we dried. Recently people have seen hotoa'o, and *vaotsevahne* (deer) on the prairies along the river, so there seems to be plenty of meat available. I must also tell you, my son, about the *ve'ho'e,* the white people who came across the great waters. They have brought great change to our village. When I was a young boy, we hunted only with arrows and dogs. These days we also use horses, guns, and many other things you will see at the trading post."

Gray Falcon couldn't wait to get going. He was proud to be Cheyenne, and he was ready to show his strength and courage to his father. This was bound to be an unforgettable day.

Painted Shield and Gray Falcon prepared for the trip. They loaded furs on the *amesto'eesenotse,* or travois. On their journey, two dogs, a mustang, and a pony would haul the sleds. It was a cold day in late spring, so father and son wore long-sleeved buckskin shirts decorated on the arm's outer seam with colorfully dyed rows of **porcupine quills.** Their buckskin leggings had similar adornments. Over their shirts, they wore heavy buffalo-skin coats to keep warm.

Morning Light, Spotted Fox, and Long Spear were helping out just as White Antelope, the village chief, rode up on a hardy black mustang. He offered Painted Shield his best wishes for the day.

"May you have a fair deal with the ve'ho'e and a rewarding hunt. As for you, Gray Falcon, don't hesitate to follow in your father's footsteps. He is among the most respected men in the village. And remember, this afternoon we will play a game. After sunset you will have the honor of listening to the words of Night Bear, the powerful medicine man. He will share his knowledge with you and a group of young people."

After waving good-bye everyone else returned home. Spotted Fox was going to visit his aunt, Evening Cloud, who had just lost two sons in a battle with the ve'ho'e. But before making his way to his aunt's tepee, he picked up his two best toys, a small doll, which he carried on his back exactly the way mothers carried their children, and his red-and-blue buffalo-skin ball. He usually took these toys with him wherever he went.

It was still early in the morning when Painted Shield and his son started out on a marked trail between hills and prairies. In the sunniest parts of the path, the snow had melted, exposing the muddy trail. On the open prairie, the wind blew incessantly. Along the way, Painted Shield stopped to point out the traditional hunting grounds. He told Gray Falcon with great nostalgia about the days when the buffalo herds gathered there, particularly during *tonoeshe'he*, or cool moon. Painted Shield explained that, since the arrival of the white people, this gathering had become rarer all the time. True, hunting was still possible for elk, deer, antelope, and many other animals. But to the Cheyenne, buffalo were still the most important animal to hunt.

After the two descended a hill, a pair of eagles appeared. Painted Shield thought this was a good omen. "Son, eagles have the ability to fly and to see farther. Their feathers are prized by our people. The eagles will guide us and protect us." Farther down the path, next to a fast-flowing stream, there were fox and beaver. Still farther a lone coyote appeared at the top of a ridge. Gray Falcon loved coyotes, so he stopped in his tracks to observe the creature. A coyote was a rare sight these days. This coyote was agile and beautiful as it trotted toward a lair of prairie dogs. Coyotes were never still—they were always exploring, often in pursuit of other animals. Their great nimbleness in deep snow enabled them to track deer and even buffalo.

After a brief stretch of forest, they came upon the trading post—a large, wooden fort in a broad clearing. As Painted Shield and Gray Falcon approached the entrance, a group of Indians was just leaving. The Indians—wearing costumes richly decorated with tiny paintings, beads, porcupine quills, fringes, elk teeth, and feathers—approached the posts to which their horses were tethered. They gave Painted Shield and Gray Falcon a friendly greeting and rode off on their horses.

Inside the trading post, there were other Indians talking quietly among themselves. Gray Falcon stared in awe at all the things the trading post had in stock. There were beads of all types and colors, shiny steel pots, sharp knives, bells, mirrors, blankets, saddles, and guns. There were also the strange foods of the white people such as sugar, flour, coffee, and alcohol. Gray Falcon had already seen the bad effects of alcohol on some of his people.

Painted Shield approached the counter and talked to the trader, a white man named McCarthy. Soon the trader laid a few bags of flour, some salt, chewing and smoking tobacco, and a gun on the counter. In turn Painted Shield showed the man beaver and mink pelts. McCarthy examined them, weighed them, and then accepted them for trade.

Gray Falcon helped his father load the goods onto the travois. They slowly made their way homeward, with plans to stop on the way to hunt for buffalo. The sun was high over the horizon, and the ground was a bit warmer. Gray Falcon felt very small in the wide-open space of the prairie. But knowing that he was in the center of the sacred mountains, the snow-covered hills, and the deep ravines of this land comforted him.

Painted Shield knew the risks of winter hunting. Even the most peaceful day could change quickly if a storm, carried by a north wind, fell on the plains. This icy wind, whipped up by **Vo'keme,** or Old Man Winter, made temperatures drop. And whirling snow transformed the landscape, causing people to lose all sense of direction.

On this day, however, conditions seemed favorable. There were no signs of change in the weather, and the sun was high in the blue sky. In a ravine to the west, not far from the trail, there was a small herd of buffalo. Painted Shield observed them intently and said to Gray Falcon, "You see, Son, we have a great advantage. Because the snow is still quite deep, the buffalo can't move quickly. Look, they're all following a leader who opens a narrow passage. They seem tired and in trouble, but it would be a mistake to underestimate them. When provoked they become extremely dangerous."

"We must surround them," Painted Shield continued, "and for this, our dogs are of great help. The buffalo will not find a way out, and their movements will be clumsy. When they huddle together, we will strike with our arrows. We may not have to follow them as we've had to in the past—the thick snow will make their escape more difficult."

After moving within striking distance on their fast and surefooted horses, Painted Shield and Gray Falcon shot a few arrows and quickly retreated to safety. Their arrows brought down three animals, and Painted Shield ended the hunt with these solemn words for Gray Falcon: "We do not kill animals to let them rot on the ground. We take only what we need, and we are grateful to all living beings that die so that we can live." Father and son then started to skin and clean the animals.

It was almost lunchtime. With the travois loaded with meat and skins, Painted Shield and Gray Falcon proceeded in single file toward home. Each hauled a heavy load on horseback. The two dogs took up the rear, each also bearing a load.

he villagers waited patiently for their return. When the hunters arrived, many young men blew their hunting whistles to welcome them. Painted Shield and Gray Falcon, exhausted and very hungry, greeted the well-wishers and headed toward Painted Shield's tepee.

Morning Light and Spotted Fox were happy to see them. Knowing they would be very tired, she had prepared a meal of drymeat, **fry bread,** turnips, and berries. The fire that burned in the middle of the tepee provided warmth and comfort after their hard work on the prairie. Painted Shield, relaxed and playful, told of the long morning's adventures. But Gray Falcon gulped down his food. He knew that many of his cousins and friends were expecting him for the game, and he didn't want to be late. After his family wished him luck, Gray Falcon hurried towards the village center, where preparations for the game were in full swing.

Gray Falcon met up with his cousins, Swift Moccasin and Brave Eagle, and some childhood friends, Yellow Beaver, Big Raven, and White Bear. Gray Falcon used to race sleds against these friends on the hills around the village. Every one of them had raced with skill and speed, but he had beat them all by bending low, supporting himself with his hands, and launching his sled at full speed from the top of the hill.

All of the players were anxious to begin. They agreed on the final details. The village medicine men had carefully crafted the balls for the game. The players also chose the playing ground—a strip of land along the Powder River, just outside the village. Many spectators had already gathered to watch the game.

In accordance with tradition, a group of young warriors stood by on horseback to maintain order. They held perfect formation and wore colorful costumes. The seams of their deerskin leggings were stitched with a brightly colored fringe of **ermine** (animal fur). Their deerskin shirts were embroidered with dyed porcupine quills. The warriors also wore feathers that waved brilliantly in the prairie wind. The ponies they rode were painted with lightning bolts and white dots of hail to suggest that the magnificent creatures were invincible. The ponies pawed and stamped at the earth, making the **dewclaw bells** on their bridles jingle and the eagle or falcon feathers decorating their tails flutter. When the warriors rode the ponies in circles, they created a whirling wheel of color, filled with flashes of black-tipped eagle feather headpieces, ornate shields, and feather-mounted lances. This group of colorful warriors drew admiration and respect from the players and the spectators.

efore long the two teams took their places on the field. The players for one team, Those Who Live Along the River, wore their hair with bangs cut short and long braids wrapped with a strip of green otter skin. The other team, the Light Tents, was Gray Falcon's team. The players wrapped strips of yellow-and-red otter skin around their long braids.

To begin the game, a young man walked to the middle of the field, stopped, turned his eyes skyward, and uttered a clear sound. With this signal, he dropped a little black ball between opposing players in center field. The strongest players from each team used their long-handled nets to try to gain control of the ball. Players soon worked the ball down the field in a series of zigzag maneuvers. The crowd shrieked its approval when the Light Tents pushed the ball toward the goal of Those Who Live Along the River.

Halfway through the game, players took a brief rest. When they resumed the game, they replaced the small black ball with a red one. One player caught the ball as soon as it hit the ground, and he immediately threw it to Gray Falcon. The crowd went wild as a free-for-all followed. But before long, Gray Falcon made a daring rush toward the other team's goal.

Painted Shield watched with great pride. His son seemed unstoppable. After dodging all the defenders, Gray Falcon tossed the ball into the goal.

At the awards ceremony that followed, the village elders stood in the center of a circle formed by the players and their supporters. White Antelope, the oldest and most influential elder, solemnly addressed the crowd.

"We have gathered on this sunny afternoon to celebrate the victory of the heroic Light Tents. We all admire the skill and loyalty both teams displayed in the competition. I am honored to participate in the festivities that will follow."

After a few drumbeats, White Antelope invited Gray Falcon to come closer. Attentive and surprised, Gray Falcon walked slowly toward the old man. A few minutes later, Gray Falcon's teammate White Bear led a pony with a long, lustrous mane through the surrounding crowd. White Bear happily handed the pony's reins to Gray Falcon, who held them tight. Gray Falcon was deeply moved by the gesture in his honor for the splendid victory and as a sign of respect.

Gray Falcon rode his pony through the village, extremely proud of his gift. He made his way to the village corral to entrust his horse to the young warrior who protects the horses from raids. When he returned to his tepee for supper, Gray Falcon noticed the strips of buffalo laid out to dry in the sun. As he lifted the buffalo-skin flap and ducked inside the tepee, the smell of stew cooking welcomed him. Morning Light stood next to the tripod and its cooking pot, stirring the stew. Gray Falcon was beside his father, who sat on a pile of soft buffalo rugs.

Gray Falcon did not linger long after dinner. He and his friends had an important meeting with Night Bear that evening. The elderly sage (wise one) was loved and respected by all the villagers. Gray Falcon entered the tepee with great deference and found a place near the fire between his friends Great Crow and White Bear.

Although very old, Night Bear was in good health. His movements were slow but steady. He was the sacred guardian of the medicine pipe.

Night Bear picked up the pipe and said with authority, "You young people must learn about our traditions. Just as when First Man became ill and his older brother taught him the ceremonial use of the pipe and a prayer to obtain relief, we use the pipe to pay homage to Ma'heo'o."

Night Bear mixed ground herbs with red-willow bark and tobacco to make **kinnikinnic.** He then pressed the mixture into the bowl of the pipe, lit it, and drew the first puff. He raised the pipe toward the sun and then lowered it toward the earth. Finally he offered the pipe to the four directions of the compass. The young men's concentration was intense.

After setting the pipe down, Night Bear spoke again. "We have acknowledged Ma'heo'o, and the night has come, I will tell you why Bear sways when he walks," he said.

"In the first days after creation, the sun used to rise, shine for a long time, and then go away, making everything dark. The daylight animals wanted the sun to shine all the time, and the night animals wanted the sun to go away forever. The two groups finally met to see what they could do about their disagreement.

Bear proposed that the two sides play a game. Then the winning side could keep the sun or throw it away. The game lasted a long time. The sun got tired of playing and so did Bear. Bear was on the night team, and he had cramps from sitting on a log for so long. So he took off his moccasins to rest his feet. The game continued. Finally the impatient sun yawned and slid out of bed on the other side of the world.

As the waking sun brightened the sky, it frightened the nighttime animals. No one had won the game yet. As the sun's light became stronger, the night animals fled. Bear was in such a hurry to escape that he put his moccasins on the wrong feet. Bear tried to keep up with the rest of the night dwellers, swaying and lurching from side to side. Since then Bear keeps rolling from side to side. And night and day take turns, in fairness to all animals."

Night Bear gathered his thoughts for a few parting words. "We know that all living creatures come from the earth and all created beings are in balance, a reflection of the perfect harmony of Ma'heo'o. Our duty is to be the keepers of this harmony. Remember this. It's late, and you should be returning to your tepees."

On the walk home, Gray Falcon reflected on the many important events of the day. He was proud to be living in this Cheyenne village. His thoughts jumped ahead to the new adventures that springtime would bring. Surely this night would be full of dreams.

Afterword

In the late 1800s, when U.S. soldiers discovered gold in the Rocky Mountains and in the Black Hills of South Dakota, prospectors rushed to the area. The discovery brought many white settlers to the area, which had belonged to the Indians for a long time. The newcomers, frightened by the Indians, persuaded the government to forcefully push them from the land. What followed was much more intense than the Indian wars of the past.

In 1864 the Massacre of Sand Creek, known as one of the most violent attacks of the time, occurred in the northeastern part of Colorado. A U.S. army detachment, led by Colonel John M. Chivington, destroyed a Cheyenne village that had been on the verge of signing a peace treaty with the U.S. government. According to the official report, about 600 hundred victims, mostly women and children, were killed.

In 1868, a few years after Sand Creek, General George Armstrong Custer attacked another Cheyenne settlement along the Washita River in Oklahoma. Once again government soldiers shot down women and children, who were desperately trying to make their way to safety. Eight years later, Cheyenne warriors, led by Two Moons, and Sioux warriors, led by Crazy Horse, retaliated. They wiped out Custer's Seventh Cavalry in the most celebrated battle of the Indian wars, along the Little Bighorn River in Montana.

But a series of incidents—including a government attack on a Cheyenne settlement along the Powder River, General Nelson Miles's call to one village on the Tongue River for surrender, and the beginning of government deportations of the Cheyenne to an Oklahoma reservation—ended Cheyenne resistance. By 1884 the government had moved the northern Cheyenne to a reservation close to the Little Bighorn River. In this area so rich in history, the Cheyenne continue living, looking forward to the future while carrying on the traditions of the past. In 1974, when the Cheyenne celebrated the 100th anniversary of the Battle of the Little Bighorn, they stressed that they were not taking joy in Custer's defeat but rather celebrating that the Cheyenne were still alive.

GLOSSARY

animist: A person who believes that objects in nature and acts of nature are filled with spiritual power.

breechclout: A square piece of hide that hangs from the waist to mid thigh and tucks between the legs.

buffalo: An imposing animal, related to cattle, that once freely roamed the grasslands of North America's Great Plains region. The Plains Indians relied heavily on the buffalo herds for food, clothing, and shelter. Because of its importance in everyday life, the buffalo also played a fundamental role in Indian mythology and rituals.

chokecherry: An American wild cherry that has a bitter taste and ranges in color from red to black.

Comanche: A Native American tribe whose territory spanned the Great Plains from Wyoming and Nebraska in the north to Texas and Mexico in the south.

conquistador: One of the Spanish explorers who conquered Mexico and parts of Central and South America in the 1500s.

Cree: A Native American tribe that lived in what came to be the Canadian provinces of Quebec, Ontario, Manitoba, and Saskatchewan.

dewclaw bells: Decorative bells strung around a horse's leg near the hoof.

ermine: A weasel found in the North American Great Plains region. The Cheyenne used ermine fur to make robes or to add decorative touches to clothing.

fry bread: A deep-fried quick bread that was a mainstay in the Plains Indian diet.

Great Plains: An area of vast, wide-open grasslands stretching eastward from the Rocky Mountains in the present-day western United States to the Missouri River.

kinnikinnic: A mixture of dried leaves, bark, and tobacco smoked by Native Americans.

Kiowa: A Native American group that inhabited what came to be the western states of Colorado, New Mexico, Oklahoma, and Texas.

leggings: Slim-fitting pants that the Cheyenne made from buck skin.

Ma'heo'o: The god, also known as Sacred One, whom the Cheyenne prayed to for help.

medicine pipe: One of the ceremonial objects the Cheyenne carved from stone or wood and adorned with feathers. During initiation ceremonies, peace talks, or other special events, village elders would fill such pipes with tobacco and herbs, light them, and pass them among the attendees.

mortar: A stone bowl in which material is pounded or rubbed with a club-shaped piece, usually also made of stone called a pestle.

nomadic: Roaming about from place to place frequently, following seasonal sources of water and food. The Cheyenne, who followed the buffalo herds across the plains, were considered a nomadic tribe.

parfleche: A rectangular, rawhide pouch that was strapped to horses and used to carry food or blankets.

pemmican: A high-energy, concentrated mass of food made from tallow and pounded dried meat.

porcupine quills: The sharp bristles that cover the back of the porcupine, a large rodent that lives in North America. The Cheyenne dyed the bristles different colors and used them to decorate clothing.

sage: A medicinal herb with grayish green, aromatic leaves. American Indians burned the sage at special ceremonies.

sinew: Tendon from buffalo or other animals that the Plains Indians used as string to bind objects together.

Sioux: A Native American group that lived in what came to be the eastern and central United States. Tribes included the Crow and the Dakota.

tallow: Animal fat that the Plains Indians mixed with other foods, such as dried meat, as a source of energy.

tepee: A cone-shaped tent made by building a framework out of pine and then draping the supports with buffalo skins. The Cheyenne and other Plains Indians left a hole in the tent's top to be used as a chimney.

trading post: A fort established by white settlers where whites and Indians met to exchange goods. Indians traded animal skins for horses and guns.

travois: A sled, consisting of two long willow poles wrapped in buffalo skins, that the Plains Indians pulled behind horses to haul goods cross-country.

tribe: A group of people and families that share the same territory, kinship, language, and traditions.

village council: A governing group composed mostly of tribal elders that decided upon issues that concerned the village as a whole.

Vo'keme: A god thought to bring winter winds and storms to the Great Plains. In present times, the Cheyenne refer to this god as Old Man Winter.

PRONUNCIATION GUIDE

amesto'eeseonotse	ahm-stoh–ih-sih-yoh-nohts
Cheyenne	SHY-ann
Comanche	koh-MAN-chee
conquistadors	kohn-KEES-tah-dohrs
hohtseme	hoht-sihm
hotoa'o	hoh-toh-wah-oh–oh
Kiowa	KIE-uh-wah
Ma'heo'o	mah-hih-oh–oh
parfleche	PAHR-flesh
Ponoma'haseneeeshe'he	poh-noh-mah–hah-sih-nih-shih–hih
Tonoeshe'he	toh-noh-ih-shih–hih
travois	truh-VOY
vaotsevahne	wah-oht-sih-vah-nih
ve'ho'e	VIH–hoh-ih (singular "man")
	vih–HOH–ih (plural "men")
Vo'keme	woh–kihm

FURTHER READING

Bonvillain, Nancy. *The Cheyennes.* Brookfield, CT: The Millbrook Press, 1996.

Braine, Susan. *Drumbeat . . . Heartbeat: A Celebration of the Pow-wow.* Minneapolis: Lerner Publications Company, 1995.

Goble, Paul. *The Return of the Buffaloes: A Plains Indian Story about Famine and Renewal of the Earth.* Washington, D.C.: National Geographic Society, 1996.

Grinnell, George Bird. *The Cheyenne Indians: Their History and Ways of Life.* New York: Cooper Square Publishers, Inc., 1962.

Hoig, Stan. *People of the Sacred Arrows: The Southern Cheyenne Today.* New York: Cobblehill Books, 1992.

Katz, Jane B. *We Rode the Wind: Recollections of Native American Life.* Minneapolis: Runestone Press, 1995.

LaDoux, Rita C. *Montana.* Minneapolis: Lerner Publications Company, 1992.

Liptak, Karen. *North American Indian Ceremonies.* New York: Franklin Watts, 1992.

Rose, LaVera. *Grandchildren of the Lakota.* Minneapolis: Carolrhoda Books, Inc., 1999.

Temko, Florence. *Traditional Crafts from Native North America.* Minneapolis: Lerner Publications Company, 1997.

Thomson, Ruth. *Indians of the Plains: Facts, Things to Make, Activities.* New York: Franklin Watts, 1991.

INDEX

About the Author and the Illustrator

Franco Meli teaches American literature at the University ILUM of Milan, Italy. His published works include *Lost Trails, Found Trails: A Collection of Short Stories By Twenty Native American Writers* and *Words in the Blood.*

Giorgio Bacchin, a native of Milan, Italy, studied the graphic arts in his hometown. After years of freelance design, Mr. Bacchin has completely devoted himself to book illustration. His works have appeared in educational and trade publications.